D1155672

THE WIRE HARP

WOLF BIERMANN

THE WIRE HARP

BALLADS / POEMS / SONGS

TRANSLATED BY ERIC BENTLEY

A HARVEST BOOK

HARCOURT, BRACE & WORLD, INC., NEW YORK

First edition
Library of Congress Catalog Card Number: 67-20306
Printed in the United States of America
Originally published in Germany under the
title *Die Drahtharfe.*

TRANSLATOR'S ACKNOWLEDGMENTS

My initial debt is to the person who took me to Biermann's apartment in East Berlin and introduced me to Biermann. It was also my introduction to Biermann's work, and I had the advantage of knowing from the start what his poems should sound like, and how, if at all, they should be sung. In the other part of Berlin I had received most friendly assistance from Klaus Schleusener and Peter Nestler. Back in the United States, I had the constant help and advice of Hugo Schmidt. Allan Miller helped me transcribe Biermann music from recording tape, so that I could work with it at my piano. The BBC invited me to record some of the songs for broadcasting in the United Kingdom. Counsel on minutiae of idiom and style was provided by Uwe Johnson and Michael Goldman.

E. B.
New York
March 1967

CONTENTS

THE BUCKOW BALLADS

PORTRAITS

BERLIN

REASSURANCES AND REVISIONS

ADDITIONAL POEMS

THE BUCKOW BALLADS

THE FIRST OF MAY

THE FIRST OF MAY

To be sung by village children

Fair is the first of May
For people come that day
The state store orders Bockwurst
And a hundred cases of beer
And students too are here
Their home is in the town
(Where such things abound)

New is the first of May
As yet there is no hay
The cows still eat the oaten straw
The writing in the cowshed's white
Though red the proclamation:
"Milk and butter here are made
And peace with every nation.
    And peace with every nation."

The Ballad of the Drainpipe Layer Fredi Rohsmeisl of Buckow
Guitar
THIS IS THE BAL-LAD OF FRE-DI ROHS-MEI-
SL DRAIN-PIPE LAYER IN THE FIELDS A-ROUND BUC-KOW GREAT RUBBER BOOTS RIGHT UP TO
BEL-LY HIS HOUSE TO THE LEFT ON FIS-CHER-KIETZ.
THERE WAS DAN-CING ONE TIME AT LE-NE KUT-
SCHIN-SKY'S THE DANCE HE DANCED WITH HIS FIAN - CÉE
WAS THE TWIST WHICH WAS NOT AL-LOW-ED O - KAY
I'VE SEEN PEO-PLE DAN-CING AND THERE'S NO DOUBT
WHAT I SAW WAS SOME-TIMES A BIT FAR OUT.
Spoken:
But
does that hurt us?
NO. (YES...)

THE BALLAD OF THE DRAINPIPE LAYER FREDI ROHSMEISL OF BUCKOW

1

This is the ballad of Fredi Rohsmeisl
Drainpipe layer in the fields around Buckow
Great rubber boots right up to his belly
His house to the left on Fischerkietz.
There was dancing one time at Lene Kutschinsky's
The dance he danced with his fiancée
Was the Twist, which was not allowed
Okay . . .

> I've seen people dancing, and there's no doubt
> What I saw was sometimes a bit far out.
> But does that hurt us? No.

2

And while he so wildly was dancing the Twist
And the music was hot and the beer was warm
Two guys came along and grabbed him by the arm
And threw him into the Taubengasse.
And then threw him clear over the fence
And beat his face in for him
And he still hadn't done a thing
And he had on his light blue suit.

> I've seen people beating, and there's no doubt
> What I saw was sometimes a bit far out.
> But does that help us? No.

3

Then Fredi Rohsmeisl went for them both
Two lefts, two rights, his aim was true
And both of them were tall guys, those two
And half of Buckow watched him do it.
Someone phoned the riot squad and it came
Fredi got beat up but good
This all the men of Buckow saw
And all the Buckow women.

> I've seen people seeing, and there's no doubt
> What I saw was sometimes a bit far out.
> But does that help us? No.

4

And now he had a trial on his neck
He was tried as a counter-revolutionary fink
Where did the state attorney find the legal right
To get him twelve weeks in the clink?
Fredi's been mad as hell ever since
And after about ten beers
He trots out his great big story for you
Over and over and over.

> I've heard people weeping, and there's no doubt
> What I heard was sometimes a bit far out.
> But does that help us? No.

5

He finds no end to it, Fredi
Is full of bitter despair
And as for social justice, well,
He thinks it's just not there.
He favors our new State
A stalwart Socialist, he
But as for the State in Buckow
He's had it—yes, sirree!

I've heard people cursing, and there's no doubt
What I heard was sometimes a bit far out.
But does that help us? No.

6

Then a few years went over the dam
And a few speeches went over the dam
There was many a change and many a surprise
Some folk could hardly believe their eyes.
And later, when the tenth Sputnik flew
The dance so hotly danced was the Twist
The state attorney—in full view
Of Fredi—tried the new dance too.

I've seen people changing, and there's no doubt
What I saw was sometimes a bit far out.
But does that help us? (Yes.)

The Ballad of the Old Women of Buckow

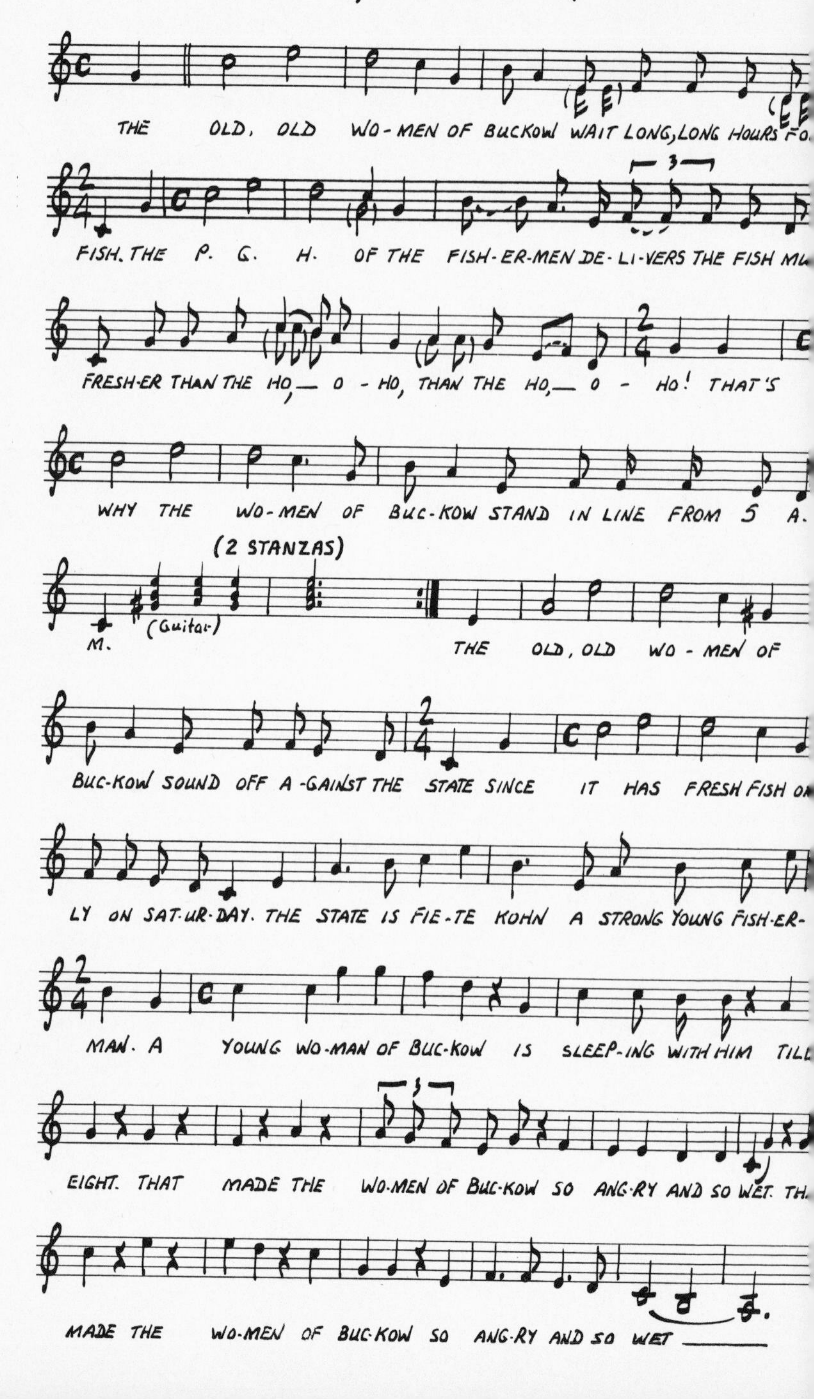

THE BALLAD OF THE OLD WOMEN OF BUCKOW

The old, old women of Buckow
Wait long, long hours for fish.
The PGH of the fishermen
Delivers the fish much fresher
Than the HO, oho, than the HO, oho!
That's why the women of Buckow
Stand in line from 5 A.M.

The old, old women of Buckow
Have a lot to say in the rain.
Of cats and mice they gabble
Of rats and other rabble:
They sound off against the HO.
That's why the women of Buckow
Stand in line from 5 A.M.

The old, old women of Buckow
Sound off against the State
Since it has fresh fish
Only on Saturday.
The State is Fiete Kohn
A strong young fisherman.
A young woman of Buckow
Is sleeping with him till eight.
That made the women of Buckow
So angry and so wet.

That made the women of Buckow
So angry and so wet.

The Ballad of the Sweet Cherry Season in Buckow

THE BALLAD OF THE SWEET CHERRY SEASON IN BUCKOW

The little room beneath the roof
Has table, chair and bed.
The sheets are fresh and white; the walls
Are blue; the floors are red.

This was in Buckow at sweet cherry time
The trees line the road as you see
This was in Buckow at sweet cherry time
Co-operatives own every tree
And on each tree a sign can be read:
THE PEOPLE'S PROPERTY IS PRO-TEC-TED!
In the night, in the night,
And especially: in the night.

The guests are young and beautiful
The hostess old and beat
And when a guest leans out the window
He sees the little street.

The street in Buckow at sweet cherry time
The trees line the road as you see
This was in Buckow at sweet cherry time
Co-operatives own every tree
And on each one this sign can be read:
THE PEOPLE'S PROPERTY IS PRO-TEC-TED!
In the night, in the night,
And especially: in the night.

A summer stillness fills the street
An old man goes for beer
Girls from the co-op pick the fruit
Until a quarter of four . . .

> The sweet, sweet cherries of sweet cherry time
> The trees line the road as you see
> This was in Buckow at sweet cherry time
> Co-operatives own every tree
> And on each one this sign can be read:
> THE PEOPLE'S PROPERTY IS PRO-TEC-TED!
> In the night, in the night,
> And especially: in the night.

When I was walking home at four
A farmer bawled me out:
"We're servicing our chicks ourselves!"
And offered to beat me up.

> This was in Buckow at sweet cherry time
> The trees line the road as see you shall
> This was in Buckow at sweet cherry time
> Co-operatives own every gal
> And on each girl a sign can be read:
> THE PEOPLE'S PROPERTY IS PRO-TEC-TED!
> In the night, in the night,
> And especially: in the night.

SMALL-TOWN SUNDAY

So, shall we go?
OK, then, let's go.
Nothing doing round here?
Nothing doing round here.
Waiter, one beer!
It's empty here.
The summer is cold.
We're getting old.
Miss Rosa has veal.
It's half past three.
Now let's go, OK?
Yeah, let's go, OK.
And is he in?
Yes, he is in.
Shall we go in?
Yes, let's go right in.
Watching TV today?
Watching TV today.
Are they showing a movie?
They are showing a movie.
Got money left?
Yeah, I got money left.
How 'bout a drink?
Yeah, let's have a drink.
So, shall we go?
OK, let us go.
Watching TV today?

Yes I'm watching TV today.

Small-Town Sunday

GOT MO-NEY LEFT? YEAH, I GOT MO-NEY LEFT.
HOW 'BOUT A DRINK? YEAH, LET'S HAVE A DRINK.
SO, SHALL WE GO? O. K. LET_ US GO.
SO, SHALL WE GO? O. K., LET'S GO. NO-THING
DO-ING 'ROUND HERE? NO-THING DO-ING 'ROUND HERE.
WAI-TER, ONE BEER! IT'S EMP-TY HERE. THE SUM-MER IS COLD.
WE'RE GET-TING OLD. MISS
RO-SA HAS VEAL (etc.) WATCHING
T. V. TO-DAY? YES I'M WATCH-ING T. V. TO-DAY.

PORTRAITS

Three years after his death
Mr. Brecht was walking
From the Huguenot Cemetery
Along Friedrichstrasse
To his theater.

On the way he met
One fat man
Two fat women
One boy.
What, he thought,
Aren't these the eager beavers
From the Brecht Archive?
What, he thought,
Are you still not finished
With all that crap?

And he smiled
His insolent-modest smile and was
Content.

Comrade Julián Grimau

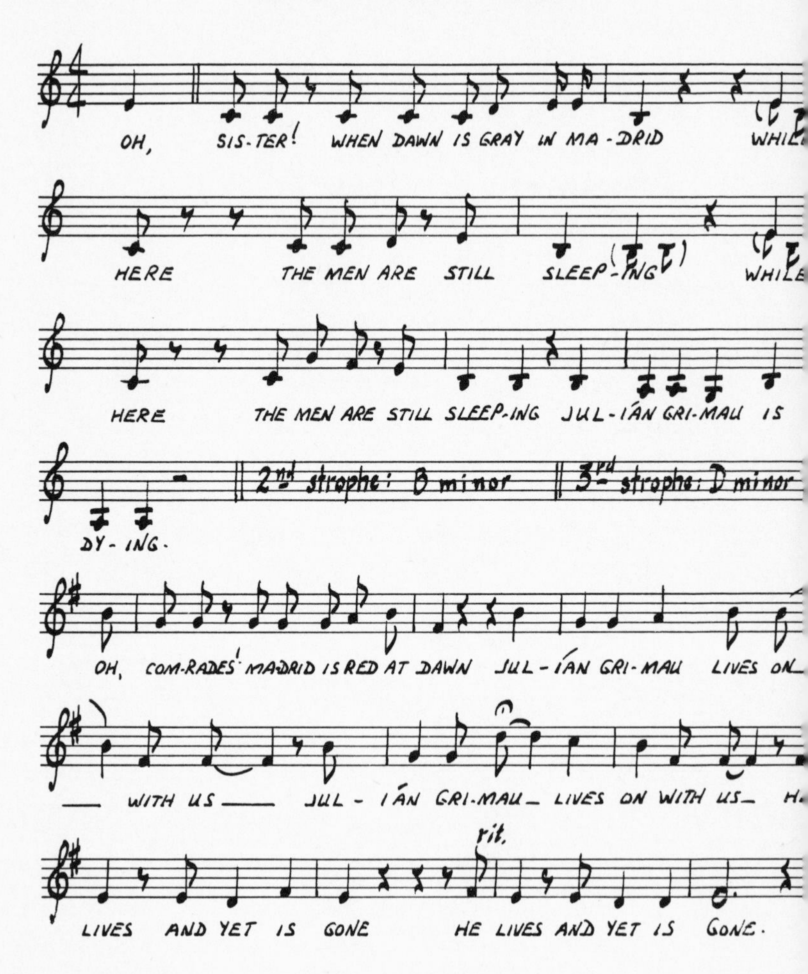

Oh, sister!
When dawn is gray in Madrid
While here the men are still sleeping
Julián Grimau is dying.

Oh, brother!
When dawn is gray in Madrid
While here the sun rises bleeding
Julián Grimau is dying.

Oh, mamma!
When dawn is gray in Madrid
Before we are reading our newspapers
Julián Grimau is dying.

Oh, comrades!
Madrid is red at dawn
Julián Grimau lives on with us!
He lives and yet is gone.

The Ballad of the Letter Carrier William L. Moore of Baltimore

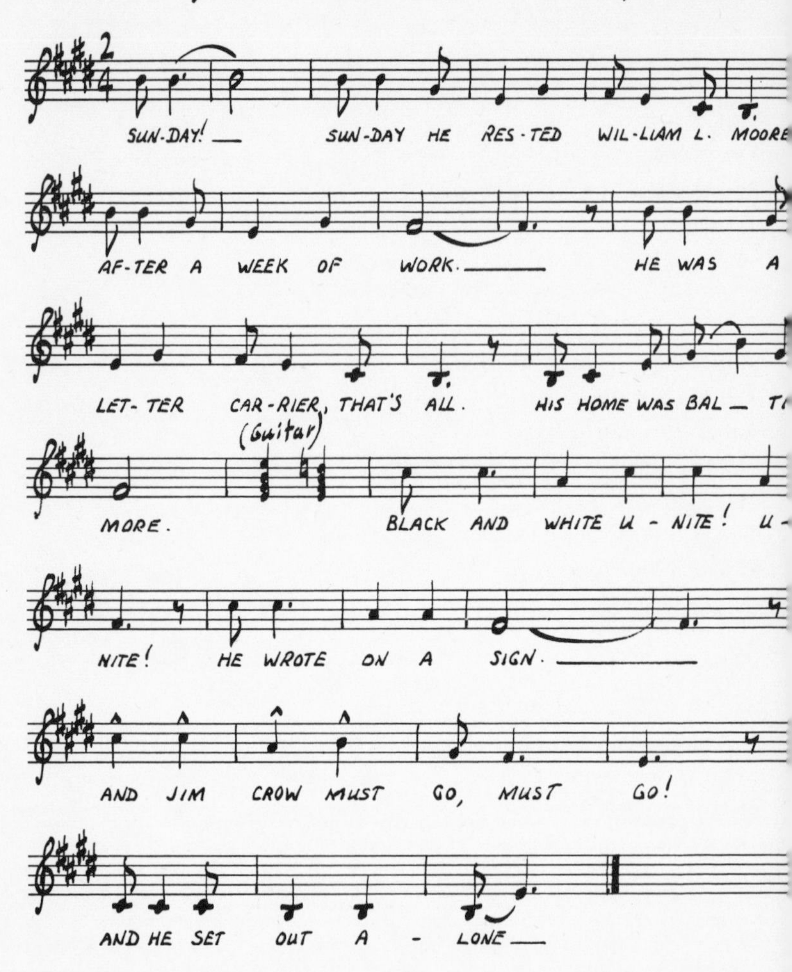

THE BALLAD OF
THE LETTER CARRIER WILLIAM L. MOORE
OF BALTIMORE

who walked alone into the Southern States in 1963.
He protested against the persecution of the Negroes.
He was shot after one week.
Three bullets struck him in the forehead.

SUNDAY

Sunday he rested, William L. Moore,
After a week of work.
He was a letter carrier, that's all.
His home was Baltimore.

MONDAY

Monday, a day in Baltimore,
To his good wife, said he:
I'm through delivering letters, my dear
It's touring the South I would be.
BLACK AND WHITE, UNITE, UNITE!
He wrote on a sign
And JIM CROW MUST GO, MUST GO!
And he set out alone.

TUESDAY

Tuesday, a day on the train going down,
Many asked William Moore:
What is the sign you got there with you?
And wished him luck on his tour.
    BLACK AND WHITE, UNITE, UNITE!
    Written on his sign . . .

WEDNESDAY

Wednesday, through Alabama that day,
William Moore went on foot.
Long is the road to Birmingham
And his feet hurt him a lot.
    BLACK AND WHITE, UNITE, UNITE! *etc.*

THURSDAY

Thursday, the Sheriff stopped William Moore
Told him: "But you are white!
"Niggers are none of your business," he said.
"Fellow, just think of the price!"
    BLACK AND WHITE, UNITE, UNITE! *etc.*

FRIDAY

Friday, a little dog followed him
Soon it was always there
And in the evening stones hit them both
But they walked on–quite a pair!
    BLACK AND WHITE, UNITE, UNITE! *etc.*

SATURDAY

Saturday, this day was frightfully hot
And a white woman came
Gave him a drink and secretly said:
"You and I think just the same."
    BLACK AND WHITE, UNITE, UNITE! *etc.*

LAST DAY

Sunday, a blue blue day, and he
Lay in the grass so green
Three red carnations, crimson as blood,
On his pale forehead were seen.
    BLACK AND WHITE, UNITE, UNITE!
    Written on his sign.
    And: JIM CROW MUST GO, MUST GO!
    And he died quite alone.
    He won't remain alone.

The Barlach Song

THE BARLACH SONG

Oh, Mother, close the windows, do,
The rain is surely coming
And yonder is the bank of clouds
That wants to fall upon us.

What is in store for us
We have so much to dread
And down to earth from heaven
Angels are falling dead.

Oh, Mother, close the doors, do,
The rats are surely coming
The hungry ones are out in front
Those that have eaten follow.

What is in store for us
We have so much to dread
And down to earth from heaven
Angels are falling dead.

Oh, Mother, close your eyes, please do,
The rain and rats are coming
And through the cracks that we forgot
They all will soon be crowding.

What is in store for us
We have so much to dread
And down to earth from heaven
Angels are falling dead.

Ballad on the Poet François Villon

BALLAD ON
THE POET FRANÇOIS VILLON

1

My elder brother Frank Villon
Lives with me as my lodger.
When people come to case the joint
Villon, the artful dodger,
Hides in the closet, solaced with
The wine he loves the most
And waits until the coast is clear.
But it's an unclear coast.

He stinks, the poet, though he must
Have smelled like rose or dahlia
Ere like a dog they buried him–
How many centuries earlier?
And when a friend's there and maybe
Three lovely girls, he'll climb
Out of the closet where he hides
And booze till breakfast time

And on occasion will sing songs
Stories and ballads many.
If he forgets the words I prompt
Him out of Brecht's *Threepenny*.

2

My elder brother Frank Villon
Suffered much persecution
From cops and churchmen who alike
Desired his execution.
Despite his age he laughs and cries
And tells tall tales and, oh,
How he will fall a-cursing at
The thought of Fat Margot!

What did she do? I ask but don't
Press my interrogations.
It's a long time ago and he
With all those supplications
With supplications Villon has
Quite often wriggled out
Of dungeon and of prison tower:
Of that there is no doubt.

With all those supplications he
Ofttimes escaped the noose.
He did not wish his neck to feel
His rear end swinging loose.

3

The vanity of rulers had
For him a smell infernal.
Into some asshole he would creep
And then make it eternal.
Oh yes, my roommate Frank Villon
He laid it on the line
So long as he had good fresh air,
Grub, and a glass of wine.

While stealing or while kissing he
Fine shameless songs would sing
As free as bird in wood; but now
He sits there stammering.
The vodka schnapps from Adlershof
Just brings on his migraine.
ND is hard for him to read
—The German gives him pain.

They taught him Latin when he was
A child at school but when
Villon got older he preferred
The speech of simpler men.

4

If Mary visits me at night
Frank Villon, for our sins,
Goes strolling on the Wall which scares
The guards out of their skins.
The bullets pass right through Villon
But not a drop of blood
Flows from the bullet holes they make,
Just red wine in a flood.

Then for a joke he makes a harp
Out of the Wall's barbed wire
The guards accompany the tune
And keep time while they fire.
And only when I am almost
Drained dry by good Marie
And she gets up to go to work
Down in the town does he

Return and cough up several pounds
Of lead with much to-do.
He curses yet is full of un-
derstanding for us two.

5

But nothing here can long be hid
And out came the whole story.
There's Order in our land just as
In Seven Dwarf territory.
There came a bang upon my door
One morning around three:
Our people's own police had sent
Three of their men to me.

They said to me, Herr Biermann, you
Are well known to us all.
You're loyal to the DDR,
You'll hear your country's call.
Is it not true–now don't be scared–
That for about a year
There has lived here a certain Frank
Fillonk who's got red hair?

He's a subversive and at night
Has offered provocation
To border guards. At this point I
Made this mild declaration:

6

"With his fresh songs he's tried to make
Of me an agitator.
I can tell you in confidence:
I do not like the traitor.
If I'd not just been reading what
Kurella has asserted
Of Kafka and the bat, I fear
I would have been subverted.

I'm glad you've come to get this crook.
He's hiding in the closet.
I gave up such impertinence
When I was—seven, was it?
I am a pious churchgoer,
A Caspar Milquetoast, I.
A docile citizen, I sing
Of flowers and softly sigh."

The cops then threw themselves upon
Poor Villon's closet door
But all they found was what he'd thrown
Up on the closet floor.

BERLIN

Ascension Day in Berlin

ASCENSION DAY IN BERLIN

The kids in the yard play happily
Princess, murderer, people's cop.
They do not have to go to school:
Today's Ascension Day.

The kids in the yard play noisily
Bedecked with rags and tatters.
They play at bride and cosmonaut
In a spaceship of cardboard.

The kids play noisily, happily.
The yard becomes a theater.
At the windows their fat mothers watch,
They are awaiting Father.

My Tenement Bride

MY TENEMENT BRIDE

My tenement bride
Lives on the sixth floor
And when the town below's still gray
Here up above there's sunshine.

My tenement bride
Sleeps by an open window.
On the window-ledge pigeons eat
My bread of yesterday evening.

My tenement bride
Has a big heart.
If I'm lonely she likes to have
A little fun with me.

A hundred stairs lead the way
To my tenement bride.
If that's not too tiring, you
Can sleep at her side.

My tenement bride
A husband should find.
But if she only finds a man
Then she does not
Then she does not
Then she does not mind.

Ballad of Bite-Crazy Barbara

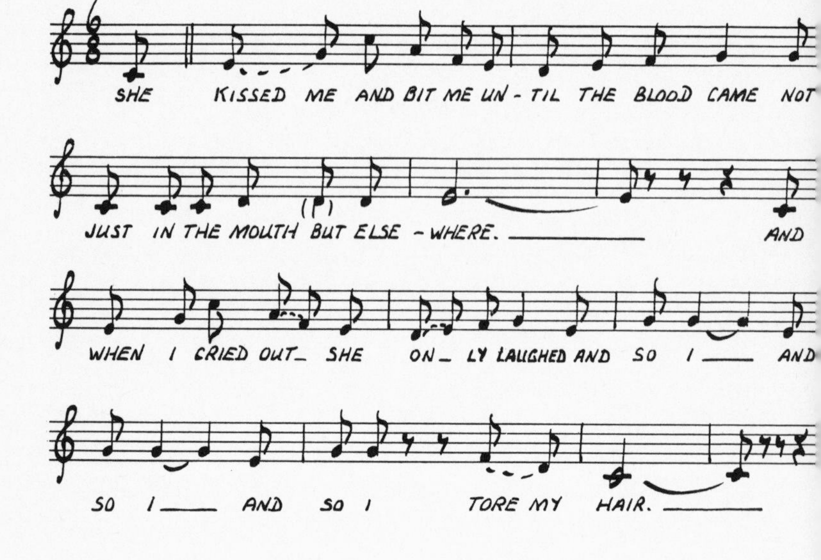

[IN THE LAST STANZA, AFTER THE PASSAGE: "I'M LOVED NOW BY GENTLE MARIE..." THERE HAS TO BE A LONG PAUSE, THE SINGING TO BE CONTINUED MUCH LATER.]

BALLAD OF
BITE-CRAZY BARBARA

She kissed me and bit me until the blood came
Not just in the mouth but elsewhere.

And when I cried out, she only laughed.
And so I
            tore my hair.

I grilled a beefsteak with pepper and salt
For Barbara's bite-crazy tooth

And as through the window she threw it, she laughed
And kissed me and
                        bit me forsooth.

And like the most abject of skirt-chasers I
Was broken upon her wheel.

But she only laughed as she mangled my limbs
That frenzied
                  feminine heel.

I'd no bit of skin or of fat left intact
From my poor bitten toes to my head

But when I said to her: So long then, my chick,
She bit in-
              to the bed.

The wounds, they healed up long ago
I'm loved now by gentle Marie.

But when I hold gentle Marie in my arms
I'm thinking of
I'm thinking of
I'm thinking of

well, not of Marie.

I went to you
Your bed was empty.
I wanted to read
And thought of nothing,
To go to the movies
And knew the film.
I went to a bar
And was alone.
I was hungry
And had a couple of drinks.
I wanted to be alone
And was among people.
I wanted to breathe
And couldn't find the exit.
I saw a woman
Who is often here.
I saw a man
Who stared into his beer.
I saw two dogs
Who did what dogs do.
I saw human beings
Who laughed at this too.
I saw a man
Who fell in the snow
It didn't hurt him
He'd been drinking so.
And over the ice
The cold made me run
Through the alleys to you
To whom all this is unknown.

AT THE EAR NOSE AND THROAT DOCTOR'S

Just throats.
A pear-shaped face
Looks across at me from under its hair.
Passing right through the many ears, noses, and throats
Our eyes find each other.

Coolness: it's the name of the veil
By which the pleasure of the eyes
Conceals itself.

The sky is full of apples
Apple pie
Apple tree
Adam's apple
Adenoidal
Adenauer.

Lots of people full of *fight*
Clung fast to Bus Number Nine
And you wore your cap so *white*
Which needs washing all the time.
And my mouth is worn away
By the pain of love's *delight.*
Every kiss has there implanted
Its own wound, and I can *write:*
"Street dust on that cap so *white.*"
And I can decide: *tonight*
I will take a little *bite*
Of you—to wash my wounds. All *right?*

But here comes the Number Nine
Which also could use a wash sometime.

BERLIN

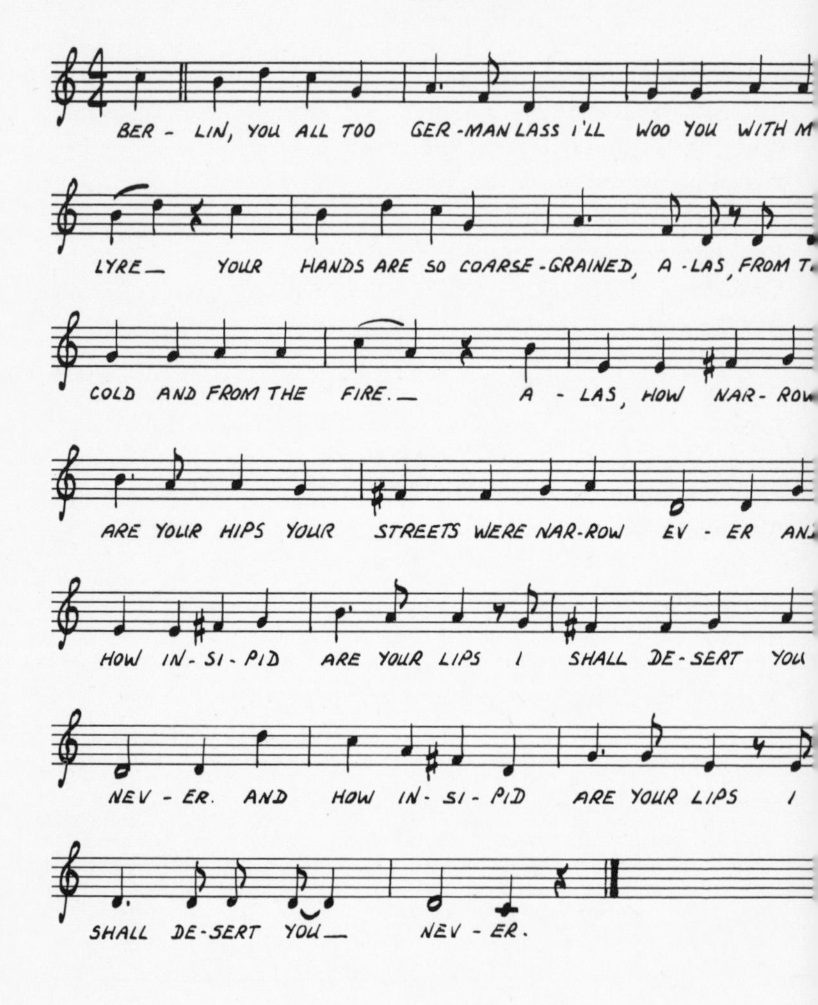
BER - LIN, YOU ALL TOO GER-MAN LASS I'LL WOO YOU WITH
LYRE— YOUR HANDS ARE SO COARSE-GRAINED, A-LAS, FROM
COLD AND FROM THE FIRE.— A - LAS, HOW NAR-
ARE YOUR HIPS YOUR STREETS WERE NAR-ROW EV - ER
HOW IN-SI-PID ARE YOUR LIPS I SHALL DE-SERT YOU
NEV - ER. AND HOW IN-SI-PID ARE YOUR LIPS I
SHALL DE-SERT YOU— NEV - ER.

BERLIN

Berlin, you all too German lass
I'll woo you with my lyre
Your hands are so coarse-grained, alas,
From the cold and from the fire.

Alas, how narrow are your hips
Your streets were narrow ever
And how insipid are your lips
I shall desert you never.

I cannot get away from you
In the West the Wall's a tough one
And in the East are my good friends
The North wind is a rough one.

Berlin, I'm coolly courting you
You're blond if not bewitching
Your sky's a rather bitchy blue
To it my lyre I'm hitching.

This morning as I lay cozily in bed
A rude bell-ringer snatched me from my sleep.
Furious and barefoot I ran to the door and opened it to
My son who
Since it was Sunday
Had gone out early for milk.

One has no use for those who come too soon.
But one drinks their milk.

REASSURANCES
AND REVISIONS

Who once bravely endured in the face of machine guns
Are afraid of my guitar. Panic spreads in all directions
When I open my jaws, and
The sweat of terror is seen on the snouts of the
bureaucrat elephants
When I treat a concert hall to my songs, truly
A monster, a plague, that's what I must be, truly
A dinosaur is dancing on the Marx Engels Platz
A backfiring shell, a dumpling stuck fast in the fat neck
Of the responsible, who fear nothing so much as
Responsibility.
Well then
would you chop your foot off
Rather than wash it? Go thirsty rather than
Drink the bitter juice of my truth, O
Man?
Undo the belt of fear that binds your chest
If you're afraid your heart might fall out if you do,
Baby!
Let it out two or three holes at any rate!
Let your chest get used to breathing freely, shouting
freely!
Put up with the internal pressure but not with the
external!
Let's really cut loose together!
We were not born to blow our great dreams stealthily
into the world
Through a handkerchief, you idiot!

Our fathers, too, were children of freedom and rebellion,
So let us be true sons of our fathers: irreverently
Roll up our rough blue shirtsleeves and sing!
shout!
get fresh and
laugh!

My soldiers shoot best
Says the General.
In the summer war
They lie among flowers
And shoot people.
At the Christmas Fair
They stand among people
And shoot flowers.
The people who've been shot down
Are gathered up by death.
The flowers that have been shot down
Are gathered up by the girl.

The ferns are shooting up.
My son is shooting up.
Ferns
Are protected by laws "for the conservation of Nature."

When at long last will our nature protect *us*
So people like us will not be shot by
People like us?

The Family Bath

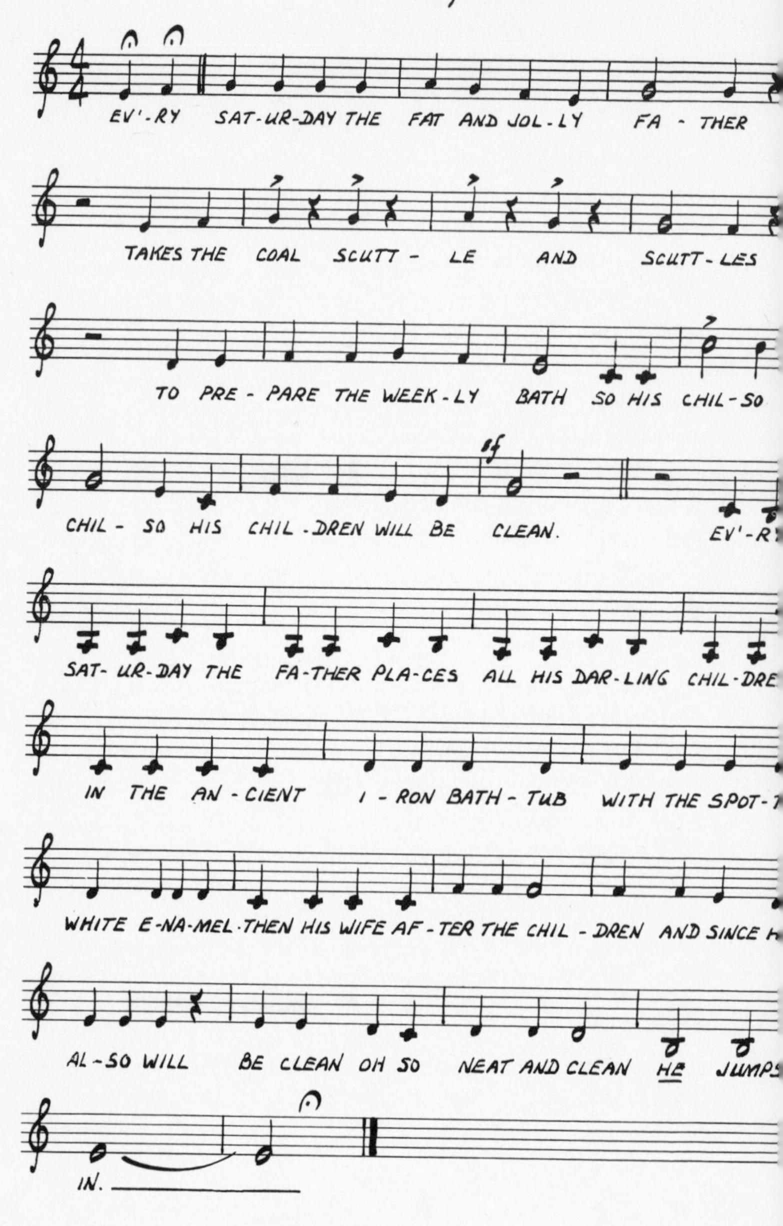

THE FAMILY BATH

Every Saturday the fat and jolly father
Takes the coal scuttle and scuttles
To prepare the weekly bath
So his chil-
so his chil-
So his children will be clean.

Every Saturday the father
Places all his darling children
In the ancient iron bathtub
With the spotty white enamel.
Then his wife after the chil-
dren and since he also will
Be clean, oh so neat and clean
He jumps in.
Every Saturday the fat and jolly father
Takes the coal scuttle and scuttles
To prepare the weekly bath
So his chil-
so his chil-
So his children will be clean.

With his good wife now he plays
Blue Mediterranean.
In the Nineteen Forties he
Spent a couple weeks down there
Major of Herr Adolf Hitler
Now he's only playing war
With his good wife in the Med-
iterranean.

    Every Saturday the fat and jolly father
    Takes the coal scuttle and scuttles
    To prepare the weekly bath
    So his chil-
                    so his chil-
    So his children will be clean.

Suddenly a shark is there,
Suddenly the wife's no more.
And the bath water that's spilling
Has turned red at Father's killing.
And his chil- chil- chil- chil- children
When they wake up in the morning
Gently open the bathroom door:
A glutted shark lies there
Mother is not anywhere
    not anywhere
        not

With the train
We learn how
To go to Grannie's.
That is fun
With the doll
We like to eat soup
Till we're full
That is fun
With the ball
We make Peter's
Bear take a fall
He's a dumb one
With the pussycats
Paul learns to scratch
Little Ann
Which is fun
With the armored truck
We learn how
Train
Doll and soup
The pussycats
And all that
Annie, Papa,
House and mouse
Are knocked flat.

There: in the middle of Germany. Stick 'em in! Stick 'em up!
The screamer The murderer The reaper Oh, God!
Into the gas, my God
No man is wholly lost Be gentle in your verdict!
Be gentle! Be gentle, citizens, Christians!
Adolf Hitler loved his dog
Adolf Eichmann loved a Jewess, the good soul

Who beheaded Germany's roses after '45?
"Rosebud rosebud rosebud red
That you always think of me."
But now the generals who brought ruin
The generals who brought ruins
Have placed a girdle about the bloody waist
Of (oh!) Germany the pale mother
"And I won't stand for it
And I *won't* stand for it!"

Everything, everything will be missing:
Soup in the pot
Salt in tears
Tears in eyes
The eye in the head
The head on the trunk
And death will be missing, yes
Even death will croak
There will be nothing left to die
The hope of death is snatched from the people

Have mercy on death
Men, have mercy
Preserve your chance of dying
If nothing else

The German language is more spiritual.
The problems of Germans are more spiritual.
Philosophy was the limber limping leg of our people.
Philosophy will teach us how to fly.

Germans! Bad conscience
Drives your philosophers into the factories
And there soot enters lungs that are already full of stale
indoor air.
And if their right hands get hit by a hammer
They quickly learn to write with the left.
If their left hands are caught in a buzz saw
They write with their mouths.

Theory–libel and eulogy–
Stands naked and ashamed
On the pedestal of the Nation
With severed hands
Oldmaidish, nice-looking.

THE POET'S AFTER-DINNER SPEECH

Thank you, Comrades
You want to see me happy.
And my eyes should encounter
Happy men.

In my songs you want to hear me
Raise high the terse tone
Of bliss. The diamond
The little diamond
You want me to enlarge
Into a block of mountains.

I'm to dish out the moment of highest pleasure
In your single-course dinner.
You shout for the red wonder cook
And when I bring you my rich foods:
Potatoes
Beefsteak
Pineapple
Olives
White bread
Garlic
Finely chopped chervil
And when I bring you baked apples from my oven
Then you shout at me
    You gluttons!

Then you hit me over the head with the asparagus
And shout for your
    Single-course dinner!
    Single-course dinner of happiness!
Every spoonful
    —unmixed joy
Every smack of the lips
    —unmixed happiness.
So you prefer to rush to the vats of bad cooks
So you prefer to lick your chops over pig food and get fat
  on it
And your fair and noble countenance, alas,
Is distorted over the pig troughs

I should sing you of the happiness of a new age
But your ears are deaf from speechmaking.
Make more happiness in reality!
Then you won't need so much Ersatz in my words.
Make yourselves a sweet life, citizens!
Then my dry wine will please you.
The poet is not a bag of sugar!
Spare yourself the humiliation of asking me to be one.

Oh, let me be the man who
Into your future surplus of happiness
Pours the bitter drop
(Spiced-cucumber, anchovies)
So that your earthly bliss won't make your palate
And your heart unresponsive!

Comrades!
Come to my table!
You! My friends!
Comrades! Forget my words, for the time being, and come!
Let us eat, and afterwards
Sing a little too.

Do Not Wait for Better Times

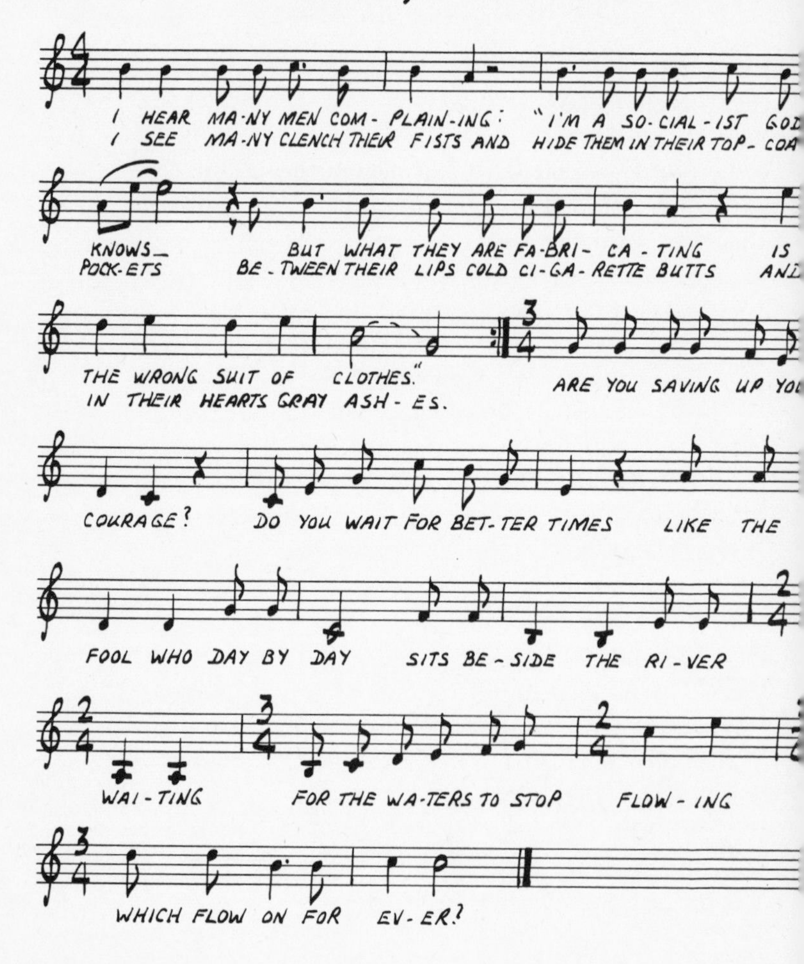

DO NOT WAIT FOR BETTER TIMES

I hear many men complaining:
"I'm a Socialist, God knows,
But what they are fabricating
Is the wrong suit of clothes."
I see many clench their fists and
Hide them in their topcoat pockets
Between their lips cold cigarette butts
And in their hearts gray ashes.

Are you saving up your courage?
Do you wait for better times
Like the fool who day by day
Sits beside the river waiting
For the waters to stop flowing
Which flow on forever?

I see many filled with hatred
Many with no hopes at all
I see many wrapped in silence
As in a woolen shawl.
Many every night are asking
What tomorrow morning's got:
Something that we can hold on to?
Then what? Then what? Then what?

Are you saving up your courage?
Do you wait for better times . . .

Many hope the river water
Very soon will cease to flow
But in springtime when the ice melts
The river starts to go.
Many tell us that these times will
Go the way the winter went,
But we must confront our problems
Confront, confront, confront!

Do not try to save your courage!
Do not wait for better times . . .

People will make sure that Social-
ism wins the victory
Not tomorrow: Now! For never
Too soon comes Liberty.
And the remedy for Social-
ism (this bit I shall roar!)
Is still more Socialism—
STILL MORE, still more, still more!

Let none try to save their courage!
Let none wait for better times
Like the fool who day by day
Sits beside the river waiting
For the waters to stop flowing
Which flow on forever
Which flow on forever

THE CROWS

When flocks of crows, a black cloth,
Rose into the pale evening sky, alas,
The thousand enchanted witches
Picked out the sky's red eye.

Crow, whither fliest thou?
—Where all are flying: to the field, to the field.

Crow, where takest thou thy rest?
—Where all are resting, in the tree, in the tree.

Crow, when dost thou cry so loud?
—When all are crying, then cry I.

Crow, when eatest thou the seed?
—When it is sown.

Crow, when dost thou die alone?
—When all things die, in the snow, in the snow.

When flocks of crows, a black cloth,
Rose into the pale evening sky, alas!
The thousand enchanted witches
Picked out the sky's red eye.

I've been seeing such things often, Comrades, of late.

1

Look at me, Comrades
With your weary eyes
With your hardened eyes
Your friendly eyes
See me dissatisfied with the age
That you hand on to me.

You speak in old words
Of the bloody victories of our class
You point with old hands to the arsenal
Of the bloody battles. Full of jealousy
I hear reports of your sufferings
Of the happiness you found in struggle behind barbed wire
Yet I myself am not happy:
I am dissatisfied with the new order.

But you stand there disappointed
Astonished
Affronted
Bitter at so much ingratitude.
You run your hands in embarrassment over your skimpy hair.

2

The present, for you
A sweet goal after all those bitter years
Is for me but a bitter beginning, and
Calls for changes. Full of impatience
I hurl myself into the battle of the classes, new ones
  which
If they don't cover the battlefield with corpses
Do cover it with sufferings.

3

Yes, many sweet fruits
Fall in our lap, and
On our heads still.

Oh, for the wedding night with the new age
For the giant embraces, oh,
And even for the deepest pain of love
Our hearts are still weak, and weak still
Are our loins.

So, many a slim young fellow
Is crushed by this great big beautiful woman
In gaudy nights of love. Yes,

Giants are needed in courage and pleasure
Giants in pain too
In fighting strength, giants. And my heart:
Red
Pale
Full of hate
Full of love
Is your own heart, Comrades,
Is only that which you have given me!

And therefore, with my impatience
Don't be impatient, old men;
Patience
For me patience is the whore of cowardice:
Buddy-buddy with laziness, she gets the bed ready
For crime.
For you, though, patience would be an adornment.
Set a good conclusion on your work
In that you leave to us
The new beginning!

1

I, I, I
Am full of hate
Am full of hardness
My head's been cut in two
My brain has been run over

I don't want to see anyone!
Don't just stand there!
Stop staring!
The Collective is on the wrong track

I am the individual
The Collective has become isolated from me
Don't glare at me so understandingly!
Oh yes, I know very well
You're waiting with earnest certitude
For me to swim
Into the net of self-criticism

But I am the pike!
You'll have to maul me, hack me to bits
Put me through a meat grinder
If you want me on bread!

2

Yes, if I were toothless
You would call me mature

If I were to smile gently
At every fat lie
You would think me
A wise man

If I were to overlook injustice
The way you overlook your wives
–You would have folded me to your bosom long ago

3

Not to call the child by its name
To smother pleasure and
To swallow pain
To walk the Middle Way
On the outermost edge of the battlefield
To call the swamp now sea, now dry land
All this you call
Reason
And do not notice that your reason is borrowed
From the brains of dwarfs
From the tails of rats
From the slits in reptiles? You

Wish to preach Communism at me
And are the Inquisition on happiness. You
Drag souls to the stake! You
Tie yearning to the wheel. You!
Get away from me with your bloated snouts!
Offended and outraged, get away from me!
Go! Shake your heads at my wrong attitude but
Go!

4

I will persist in truth
I, the liar

5

I love all of you:
This I set my name to
Rain, hail, or storm
My love for you is warm
But now please leave me alone
On my wrong track
Cut off from the Collective
Yes, I have strange bedfellows
My bedfellow is my wife
And she knows where my heart is

Ballad of the Man

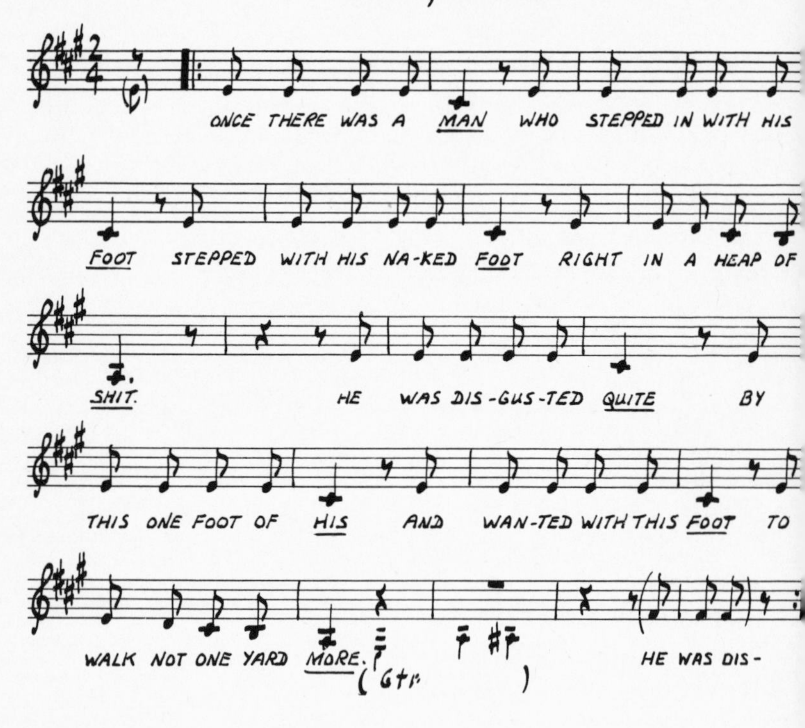

[AND SO ON, AND SO FORTH, EACH TIME TRANSPOSED BY A WHOLE TONE.]

Once there was a man
Who stepped in with his foot
Stepped with his naked foot
Right in a heap of shit.

He was disgusted quite
By this one foot of his
And wanted with this foot
To walk not one yard more.

There was no water there
To wash this foot of his
For this one foot of his
There was no water there.

So this man took an axe
And hacked that foot right off
That foot he hacked right off
Hurriedly with his axe.

He hurried overmuch
It was the cleaner foot
It was the wrong foot that
He hurriedly chopped off.

*Who cut off both his feet with his own hands.

Then he got in a rage
And so made up his mind
To chop off with his axe
The other foot as well.

The two feet both lay there
The two feet both grew cold
Chalk-white before them sat
Upon his rump the man.

The Party, it has chopped
So many a foot off
So many a good foot
The Party has chopped off.

Yet, as is not the case
With the above-mentioned man,
In the Party's case sometimes
The foot grows on again.

SELF-PORTRAIT ON A RAINY SUNDAY IN THE CITY OF BERLIN

Equipped with the knives of reason am I
Cool logic guides my bullets round the corners
Arrogance and sophistry smooth the way for me
Inexorably my doubts torture this city of stone
More insolently, more nervously
I swim in safety even in its drainpipes
And my scorn climbs higher than the radio towers
I can be bought with the currency of truth, payable in
cash
In the bunkers of my skepticism I sit immune
To the radiance of the great obscurantists
And the hatred of yesterday shields me from the storm
Of tomorrow. Take note that I am equipped

And yet I am also exposed, quite often in fact
Again and again I lie there freshly slaughtered
Torn apart under the wild sky of the neighborhood
Butcher hooks are driven into my belly
Whaling factories float in my eye
On my tongue lies the hope of the hopeless
Feebly my wild dreams flow in the end
Into the shambles of your schools and offices
Sausage machines greedily swallow my remains
The countryside waits hungrily on the edge of the sea of
houses
And the great wet city licks its chops
Over the well-earned Sunday roast Biermann

Nothing To It

NOTHING TO IT

When I'm on fire
When I'm on fire
    I reach down a cloud from heaven
    And wring it out over me.
Icy shower.
                    Nothing to it.

When I am freezing
When I am freezing
    I reach down the sun from heaven
    And stick it under my coat.
Little oven.
                    Nothing to it.

When I'm at her place
When I'm at her place
    Clouds come floating down from heaven
    Down with the clouds rolls the sun.
That's what love's like.
                    Nothing to it.

When I am tired
When I am tired
    I reach God down from His heaven
    And have Him sing me a song.
Angels shed tears.
                    Nothing to it.

When I am plastered
When I am plastered
    I go down to see the Devil
    And I buy Stalin a beer.
Poor old fellow.
            Nebbish.

When I'm dead I'll be a
When I'm dead I'll be a
    Border guard and I'll keep watch on
    The border 'twixt heaven and hell.
Show your passport!
            Nothing to it.

ADDITIONAL POEMS

GERMANY:

A WINTER'S TALE

(Part One)

In the German December from East Berlin
To West Berlin flowed the Spree
And I floated in a railway train
High over the Wall and away.

And soaring over the bloodhounds there
And all that barbed-wire mess
My mind filled up with wonder
And my soul with bitterness.

My heart filled up with bitterness
At the comrades true I've got
For ever so many a man who went
This way on foot had been shot.

Many have thrown their youthful flesh
On the wire and the mines.
The riddled bucket leaks when the sub-
Machine gun barks from behind.

Not every man is so well built
As the poet Frank Villon
Who got away with a few red spots—
Just winestains, says the song.

My mind's eye saw a cousin of mine
The impertinent Heinrich Heine
Who swam to Germany from France
With the aid of Father Rhine-a.

I could not but think of what plainly occurred
In the hundred years, to wit:
That Germany, gloriously unified,
Again went and got itself split.

So what? The whole wide world has made
This East and West division.
Yet Germany has somehow contrived
Once more to maintain its position.

Its position as the whole world's ass
So weighty and so fat.
The hairs inside the crack are made
Of wire (and barbed, at that).

Even the hole (I mean Berlin)
Is split by a like duality:
In which we see how human skill
Can put to shame biology.

And when the bellies of the great
Of all the world give pain
The stink and din in Germany's
Tremendous. I'll explain:

Each part of the wide world has its own
Part of the German po-po.
The biggest part's West Germany.
With reason good, I know.

And so with German industry
To save embarrassment
West Germans polish and perfume
The German excrement.

And they have managed to succeed
Where alchemy failed, I'm told:
In German shit has now been found
The formula for gold.

The DDR, my Fatherland,
However, is very clean
And a return to Nazi ways
Is nowhere to be seen.

With the hard broom of Stalin we
So rubbed our bodies down
The backside now is scratched all red
That formerly was brown.

Legend of the Soldier in World War III

LEGEND OF THE SOLDIER IN WORLD WAR III

When morning murder roused his lust
The sleep he slept was grand:
He lay on his gal, and she could see
The stars of the Fatherland.
Atomic rockets fell like hail
Out of a clear bright sky.
Most of the bombs fell far too late
There was nothing left to die.

Now it is winter time
Long and broad evenings
Mourn in the snow.
While love lasts we shall find,
Karen, though cold the wind,
That all is well.

The earth was one great ship of death
One big round open sore
The stars in the sky weren't beautiful now
No one saw them any more.
The angels' wings were all burned off
The Lord God's beard was burned
For lack of souls the Day of Judgment
Had to be adjourned.

Now it is winter time
Long and broad evenings
Mourn in the snow.
While love lasts we shall find,
Karen, though cold the wind,
That all is well.

And one molecule from the gal's behind
And one from the soldier's head
Were standing side by side until
The firestorm killed them dead.
And had the soldier given his gal
A child instead of a war
The heart of the earth would be beating now
And war would be laughed to scorn.

When summer comes shall we
Karen, at last be three
Among the flowers?
War shall itself be dead
And when the cherries are red
All will be well.

MORNING DICTUM OF GENERAL KY

A government that has nothing more to fear
Than the people
Can last a long time, as long as
The people fears nothing more
Than the government.

But finally the government passed a law
That all men are
Happy
Breaches of this law
Were punished with death
Soon
There were really only
Happy men

QUESTION AND ANSWER AND QUESTION

They say one cannot change
Horses in midstream
Good. But the old ones have drowned already

You say that the admission of our mistakes
Is useful to the enemy
Good. To whom is our lying useful?

Many say: In the long run Socialism
Is quite unavoidable
Good. But who's putting it through?

NOTES

THE BALLAD OF THE OLD WOMEN OF BUCKOW

PGH: the initials stand for *Produktionsgenossenschaften des Handwerks,* words which mean "production co-operatives of crafts."
HO: stands for *Handelsorganisation,* "trading organization," the name attached to government-owned food shops in East Germany. And, of course, the exclamations "Ho!" and "Oho!" exist in German as well as in English.

THE BALLAD OF THE SWEET CHERRY SEASON IN BUCKOW

Co-operatives: Landwirtschaftliche Produktionsgenossenschaften, which means "agricultural production co-operatives."

COMRADE JULIÁN GRIMAU

Julián Grimau was a Communist who was executed under the Franco regime—at dawn, April 20, 1963.

BALLAD ON THE POET FRANÇOIS VILLON

ND: initials of *Neues Deutschland,* Communist newspaper, written in the language of functionaries.
DDR: Deutsche Demokratische Republik, or German Democratic Republic.
Kurella: Alfred Kurella (born 1895), a man who has held various important cultural posts in East Germany during the past dozen years. Attending a Kafka conference in Prague in 1962, he took the anti-Kafka side, and later wrote that, if one swallow does not make a summer, this swallow—Kafka—was in any case a bat.

AT THE EAR NOSE AND THROAT DOCTOR'S

In German, *die Mandel* is either the almond or the tonsil. Forced to seek the name of something in the throat which was also the name of a fruit, the translator has settled for *Adam's apple.* (To fit the new pattern, a *hazel nut* becomes a *pear.*) Adenoids suggests Adenauer (and vice versa, though the words Biermann worked with are *Mandel* and *Fernandel*).

RHYME TRAUMA

This poem is based on German rhymes which cannot be duplicated in English.

THE SINGER'S INAUGURAL ADDRESS

Like the English word "man," the German word *Mensch* can be either ultra-dignified or quite slangy and low. However, in the present context, the translator has thought it necessary to translate *Mensch,* in one instance, as "baby."

THE FAMILY BATH

Biermann plays a verbal trick that cannot be duplicated in English. In German the first syllable of the word for cleanliness (*Sau*berkeit) means *pig.* By pausing after this first syllable, Biermann is able, while talking of cleanliness, to indicate that he thinks the father is a pig. The word play in the English is, perforce, different—it is by way of using the first syllable of *children* to suggest the blood-*chill*ing.

LAST VARIATION ON THE OLD THEME

Stick 'em in!: This phrase translates *Steck ein!* which has been attributed to General Trettner, at the time this poem was written head of the West German army. On being asked about the possibility of mines being placed at the border between East and

West Germany, Trettner is supposed to have said, "Stick 'em in." (He denies it.)
Pale mother: the phrase, as applied to Germany, is taken from the opening phrase of Brecht's poem "Deutschland": *O Deutschland, bleiche Mutter.* The passages in quotation marks are from Goethe's well-known poem, "Heidenröslein."

THE POET'S AFTER-DINNER SPEECH

Single-course dinner: the phrase translates *Eintopf,* a name for a single-dish meal which was enjoined on everyone on certain days in Hitler Germany.

RECKLESS ABUSE

Yes, I have strange bedfellows: Here, one pun has replaced another. The German reads: *Ich liege eben schief/Ich lieg bei meiner Frau,* which in an unpunning, literal translation would read: "I am off the track/I lie (sleep) with my wife."

BALLAD OF THE MAN

The translator has aimed at the metrical primitivity of nursery rhyme, but in the original a particular nursery rhyme is alluded to, that begins: *Es war einmal ein Mann,/Der hatte einen Schwamm . . .* (The same nursery rhyme seems to lurk in the background of *Brigitte.*)

GERMANY: A WINTER'S TALE (PART ONE)

Unpublished in *Die Drahtharfe,* it appeared in *Neuss (sic) Deutschland,* 8 May 1965, a sort of German *Private Eye,* published in West Berlin until forced out of business by the Establishment in early 1966. It is the first part of what is reported (1967) to be a very long poem.

For German readers, the principal allusion of the title is not to Shakespeare but to Heine.

LEGEND OF THE SOLDIER IN WORLD WAR III

Unpublished in *Die Drahtharfe,* the German text has been transcribed from a tape recording. As the title suggests, this song is a kind of sequel to a poem in Brecht's *Manual of Piety,* "Legend of the Dead Soldier"; and the "gal" of Biermann's opening lines might possibly be the "half-uncovered gal" of Brecht's seventh stanza.

Wolf Biermann, born 1936, East German poet and balladeer, wrote his first poems and songs in the late 1950's and became known to a small circle in the early 1960's. He sang and recited his bitingly satirical verse in rented halls, universities, and writers' clubs in both Germanys, but was unable to have them published in East Germany where he lives. A first volume of his poetry was published in West Berlin by Verlag Klaus Wagenbach in autumn, 1965, with the title *Die Drahtharfe* (The Wire Harp). A few months later, Biermann came under heavy attack in the East German party newspaper, *Neues Deutschland.* Biermann has since been forbidden to perform and to travel, even in Communist countries, and no book of his has appeared in East Germany or any of the other Communist countries.

However, Wolf Biermann does not consider himself an anti-Communist. He is the representative of the young, who believe in the necessity of free expression of criticism, and consider him a dramatic symbol of a new age.